I0697052

A LIBERTARIAN'S JOURNAL

A LIBERTARIAN'S JOURNAL

VOLUME 1

BY

FRANC TURNER

A Libertarian's Journal, Volume 1. Copyright © 2021 by Franc Turner. All rights reserved. Printed in the United States of America. No part of this book may be reproduced, distributed, or transmitted in any form or by any means, including photocopying, recording, or other electronic or mechanical methods, without the prior written permission of the publisher, except in the case of brief quotations embodied in critical reviews and certain other noncommercial uses permitted by United States of America copyright law.

The opinions and perspectives in this book are Franc Turner's alone, and may or not be the opinions or perspectives of individuals mentioned or presented within it.

Published by Steve Cameron Productions. Editing, cover, and book design by Franc Turner and Steve Cameron.

stevecameronproductions.com

"Congress shall make no law respecting an establishment of religion, or prohibiting the free exercise thereof; or abridging the freedom of speech, or of the press; or the right of the people peaceably to assemble, and to petition the Government for a redress of grievances."

-–First Amendment of the Constitution of the United States

"We've now sunk to a depth at which restatement of the obvious is the first duty of intelligent men."

–George Orwell

Dedicated to my parents, John and Carolyn, who always inspired me to stand up for what I know is right and just in this world.

CONTENTS

CONTENTS

FOREWORD

BY DONALD JEFFRIES

I am not a Libertarian, per se, but I still have many Libertarian instincts, and certainly support civil liberties and an honest money system, and oppose our disastrous interventionist foreign policy and wasteful, fraudulent government spending. Ron Paul remains one of my heroes.

Franc Turner's *A Libertarian's Journal* is a critical and insightful look at the madness that has engulfed this country, and the whole world, over the past year and a half. It is a chronicle of events in real time; Turner relates the increasingly surreal policies and pronouncements and expresses his understandable opposition to it all. It was indeed, in Turner's words, "an ominous, confusing, stressful, freakshow of a year."

Turner asks the questions here that real journalists would ask, if we had a truly free press in this country, and not the obviously state-controlled media that has fueled this Plandemic with nonstop disinformation and fear porn. You don't have to call yourself a Libertarian to be concerned about the monstrous authoritarianism that has taken over this country. The authorities must not be questioned. If you question them, we will send the "fact checkers" after you. Or suspend your social media accounts. Or "cancel" you entirely, so that you not only become ostracized by your peers who are sound asleep, but lose the means of making a living.

All this is not happening because of a random, deadly virus. As Turner notes, "the government has orchestrated it to be this way." This entire psyop has been produced by the combined forces of our horrendous Medical Industrial Complex, establishment scientists and eugenicists like software monopolist Bill Gates, corrupt politicians, and laughable talking heads in the media. And the same public that bought the 9/11 fairy tale and countless other official lies, clings to their double masks and lines up for "boosters" to counter the never ending "variants."

As Ron Paul noted early on in this psyop, when you give government new powers, they never give them back. Things are never going back to "normal." Our leaders know that they can invoke health concerns, and the masses will not only obey every nonsensical measure they devise, but relinquish what's left of their rights. Families are being divided over a virus that is, to quote Dr. Roger Hodkinson and others, "just a bad flu." If the authorities start offering bounties to turn in the Unvaccinated, look for our vaccinated loved ones to be ready and willing.

Like some great works in the past, such as Thomas Paine's *Common Sense*, and General Smedley Butler's *War is a Racket*, Franc Turner's *A Libertarian's Journal* is a slim volume. But it is packed with common sense and intelligent observations. This is a book that needs to be read by all Americans. Especially now, when we are dealing with the Greatest Psyop in the History of the World.

Donald Jeffries is a best-selling author and radio personality from the United States. Some of his books include *Survival of the Richest: How the Corruption of the Marketplace and the Disparity of Wealth Created the Greatest Conspiracy of All* (foreword by Naomi Wolf), *Bullyocracy*, and *Hidden History: An Expose of Modern Crimes, Conspiracies, and Cover-Ups in American Politics.*

INTRODUCTION

BY FRANC TURNER

March of 2020 through March of 2021 was an ominous, confusing, stressful, freakshow of a year, pretty much for everyone around the globe. It was a time in which many of the fundamental aspects of society, institutions, human interaction, business, and civilization itself drastically shifted in ways that many people have struggled to come to terms with, and many more have strangely come to embrace... especially those in positions of power and authority, and those who look to them for guidance and leadership.

It was a time in which people's thoughts, behaviors, and outlook on life were heavily shaped, molded, and solidified by the barrage of apparent historical events, tragedies, and existential threats to life, limb, and health. Ordinary people's animosity towards one another seemed to have grown exponentially.. at home, in the streets, and in the world of cyberspace...

Every social media thread argument ever:

"I feel that the issue here is **insert random contrarian comment here, nitpicking inconsequential inconsistencies, while simultaneously and unsuccessfully persuading anyone who doesn't already agree, with superfluous confirmation-biased stats**, because it is all the fault of **insert unfavorable political figurehead here**, because facts are facts.

Continues to argue a moot point, going around in circles for comment after comment until one or the other simply leaves the thread"

World events, past and present, and how they affect the world that comes after, have been a fascination of mine for as long as I can remember. I've always tried to view the world beyond on a superficial level. I look for the underlying meanings, reasons, and motivations of actions.. and I, generally speaking, don't accept things at face value unless there's evidence to demonstrate that there's no need to dig deeper.

I studied psychology in my schooling years, and learned about the conditioning of behaviors and how easy it is for social engineers to manipulate people into eliciting the behaviors they view as "desirable." On my own time, I've studied history, governments, politics, and patterns of atrocities carried out by those in positions of authority.

I'm a hobbyist sleight of hand cardist, so I'm well aware of perception and misdirection. While I use the sleight of hand with playing cards to create neat effects, governments seem to use sleight of perception to get everyone focused on other things while they screw us over on a regular basis.. and actually get most people to beg for it.

I'm also a musician, artist, and writer. I think I've just always had a knack for seeing through b.s., fakes, and people who prey on others' vulnerabilities. I am an adamant advocate for the free will of a human being. I'm totally opposed to coercion, those who take advantage of others, and instances of true injustices and abuses of power. I believe in self-ownership, self-reliance, and self-governance.

Combine all this, and it's no wonder that I have so much skepticism towards those who wish to control every aspect of our existence. It's just not in me to be a silent little zombified drone. Always remember that no one can take away our humanity, despite how hard they try to knock it out of us.

INTRODUCTION

This book is dedicated to that idea. It is a year's worth of my thoughts, observations, and commentary on the events that transpired over the course of last year. I hope, at the very least, it gets you to ponder and consider concepts and perspectives, that you might not have been exposed to before. With these words, I am not giving advice to anyone on how to live their lives. People have to choose what's best for themselves, their families, and their communities. I'm only trying to get people to think.

Enjoy!

I

JOURNAL ENTRY:
MARCH 11, 2020

Anyone else find it odd that the governments of the world agree on absolutely nothing; but when it comes to what should be done about a novel pneumonia virus (aka- Coronavirus), practically every one of them are on the same page about what should be implemented: contingency plans for random martial law anywhere on the globe at a moment's notice, so that no one in any of the euphemistically Orwellian "containment zones" can go anywhere or do anything unless those in power say you can. No one else thinks it kind of sets a worrisome precedent that if something like this (which apparently, for the majority of people, isn't a significant health risk) can cause the governments of the world to respond such as this, with such coordination and cooperation... then what exactly will their response be when something more serious comes along?

There have been dozens of fear mongering "viral outbreaks" which the media has conditioned the public to fear over just the past few decades. What should cause concern, however, is the agendas which are being rolled out, as this virus (covid 19) is used as the excuse..

II

JOURNAL ENTRY:
MARCH 15, 2020

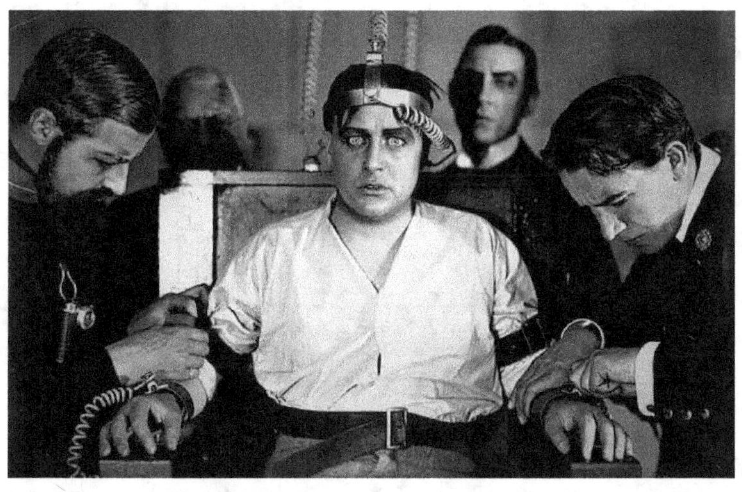

Anyone out there familiar with the Milgram Experiments? They were a series of replicated studies which took place in the 1960's to see if normal people could be made to commit (what they believed to be) heinous acts against their fellow human beings simply because an authority figure told them that they "must continue."

The test subjects were made to believe that it was a study on "the effects of pain on learning," and that the subjects were in control of what they believed to be an "electrical shock delivery" to the other participant (actor) if a question was answered incorrectly. The "voltage" was increased each time the "learner" got an answer wrong. The "learners" (actors) would scream out in pain as the shocks were delivered. They, the actors, would plead that they had heart conditions and beg the test subjects to stop. The authority figure in the room would simply tell the subject in a calm manner, "Please continue," or "You must continue," or "For the sake of the experiment, you must continue." Many participants continued until they believed the learner was deceased.

While the nature of the experiment is rather shocking (pardon the pun) in and of itself, what's even more alarming is the tangible "power" that those in perceived positions of authority can yield. The vast majority of the actual test subjects continued what they believed to be the torturing of their fellow participants well past the point where they were personally uncomfortable with what they were being told to do, merely because someone in a lab coat gave them "orders" to carry it out. Well over half the subjects even delivered what they believed to be the final, fatal shock to the "learner." They didn't have to have a gun held to their head, nor did they need any kind of threat towards their own safety in any way. This experiment demonstrated that all is needed for most people to commit violent or even murderous acts is simply the request of an authority figure in uniform.

When these experiments were conducted decades ago, the percentage of ordinary people who delivered the final shock was 65%. Modern day replications of the experiment have shown that even higher percentages of participants will deliver the final shock.

With everything that's been happening in the world, I think these experiments should be a good reminder to people that it is EXTREMELY easy for those in power to get ordinary people to do anything and everything they want… simply because they say it… "You must."

Sure, take precautions against illness. But, also, take a look around at how quickly all aspects of life are now under the commands of those "authorities" who've granted themselves the "power" to regulate all aspects of society. This isn't about the virus, folks.

III

JOURNAL ENTRY: MARCH 18, 2020

When the government begins giving out money to the American people... and when I say "give money," I mean skimming off a tiny fraction of the money that the government stole from your pockets in the first place and throwing it back at you... and when they begin bailing out the airlines, the cruise lines, the oil and gas companies, the fracking industry, the stock market, etc... while small businesses and ordinary citizens are left dependent on the scraps the government gives them to pay bills and buy groceries, unless they wanna starve... ironically, these actions that are going to take place will make Donald Trump the most socialist president this country has ever had. And it'll be interesting to watch the voters of this country, both Democrat and Republican, as this all comes to fruition. Those who have longed for this kind of social democracy will get all the things they've asked for over the past several years and then some, and yet the figurehead of Donald Trump will still be the most despised human to have ever existed to them. Conversely, those who have said that socialism is the most evil system that the world has ever seen, will suddenly praise all the actions put into place by their "Make America Great Again" puppet master. And, my goodness, will the Facebook arguments be excruciating to watch... seeing Republicans defend Socialist Trump, and seeing Democrats despise Socialist Trump.

The reason why anyone is in hardship right now is because the government has orchestrated it to be this way. They have literally taken control of all aspects of your life and are making you all dependent on them... when they've stolen the majority of what you earn in the first place... they magically create $1.5 trillion out of thin air here, and another $850 billion there... and tell you all that you can't congregate together, or keep your place of business open, or go anywhere unless they say so. So, congratulations America, all of your decisions will be made for you from now on, and you can continue to pretend that voting for this president or that president is going to make a difference in people's lives. So take your slave payments, your complacency payments, your obedience payments... and keep pretending that you're free. Or we could all stop paying our income taxes and tell the system to go fuck itself. Ask yourself, "If they can create money out of thin air, then why do they need to take money out of my paycheck?" The answer to this, and the answer as to why governments around the world are doing what they're doing right now is one simple word... Control.

IV

JOURNAL ENTRY:
MARCH 25, 2020

Tips and Tricks for the Modern Day
Governmental Authoritarian A-hole...

Step 1: Get people accustomed to the
idea of potential worldwide pandemics
via bi-yearly media propaganda for two
decades straight.

Step 2: Condition people to view those who question the idea of mandatory inoculations as being intellectually inferior, moronic, stupid, unscientific, and a threat to the health and well-being of others... via constant bombardment through social media, television programming, Netflix series, news anchors, popular movies, celebrity endorsements, etc. ***Make sure to stifle dissenting voices via insults, Twitter mobs, Facebook trolling, and pathological regurgitation of political talking points.. until no one brings up differing, uncommon, or uncomfortable opinions anymore***

Step 3: Unleash (or look the other way) as an amped up pneumonia virus, which has the potential to devastate vulnerable populations, spreads quickly throughout the world.. as "slow to respond" governments quickly take over all business, education, entertainment, industry, travel, commerce, and media in order to try to "contain" said virus.

Step 4: Get people accustomed to the idea of perpetually mandated self-isolation, shortages, rationing of goods and health services, monetary hardships, financial and social uncertainty, governmental decrees, and governmental "solutions."

Step 5: Introduce vaccine for said

virus, and mandate that every human being in the world must take it... if they want to have a business, go to school, attend concerts, go to work, go on vacation, open a bank account, or speak on a media platform... as the previous years' societal conditioning will pressure most to fall in line. And those who don't comply will be forced to comply, "for the safety of others," despite what the first point of the Nuremberg Code states.

Step 6: Enjoy the newly created populations, docile and critically unthinking, who bend at the whim of any new legislation, mandate, decree, order, etc... and who will defend the State at any cost (and beg for each and every one of their rights to be taken away), in order to maintain what they see as a "stable" society.

And voila!!

V

JOURNAL ENTRY:
APRIL 12, 2020

2019 was a year in which faith and trust in government and media was probably the lowest it had ever been. Viral news stories which became the headlines of the week were then shown to be completely skewed (and sometimes completely fabricated) narratives. For example: Walls vs. Open Borders, Russia Russia Russia, Red Flag laws, Maga Hats vs. Blue-No-Matter-Who, Impeachment Drama, Jussie Smollett. Trump Kids vs. Native American Standoffs, Fake Viral Challenges, etc.

Then there was the whole Jeffrey Epstein situation. This was quite the interesting story, and a rather unique one, at that. This was because no matter what political affiliation someone was ascribed to, no matter how old or young a person was, no matter if someone follows politics or not; practically every single person on planet earth knows that Jeffrey Epstein didn't kill himself, and everyone also knows WHY he didn't kill himself. The issue of highly prominent political, governmental, celebrity, royalty, or business personalities all being tied to this guy seemed to raise quite a few red flags about the true nature of those who are governing this world. And, again, everyone knows WHY these VIP's were tied to Epstein… ergo, why all these people benefited from Epstein's subsequent "suicide" *Hysterical Laughter*. Sorry, I can't keep a straight face when I say that out loud.

2019 was also a year when people were no longer really paying any attention to the War on Terror, or anything relating to it. People had grown desensitized to such a degree that words like "Al Qaeda," or "Isis," or "Terrorist," or "Terrorist Threat" no longer struck fear into the world population's collective psyche, nor did it cause them to change their way of life due to the fear of being a victim of a terrorist attack… like they did in the years that followed September 11, 2001.

Then, along comes 2020. The year of hindsight. The year of 20/20 vision. The year of worldwide pandemic. Suddenly, and despite the fact that government and media had given the people of this world every single reason under the sun to be skeptical of their intentions, plans, suggestions, policies, agendas, etc; all of a sudden, the only thing needed for the governments to gain everyone's silent obedient consent was one simple word: Coronavirus.

Suddenly, everyone is looking the right way again, from a power and authority perspective. They have managed to corral everyone on planet earth with neat little government-approved terminology like social distancing, six-foot rule, shelter-in-place, stay-at-home, wear a mask, follow the arrows, and wash your hands, wash your hands, wash your hands. Did I mention, "Wash your hands?" The "Flat Earth Society" has been replaced by the "Flat Curve Society": a society in which pretty much everyone has developed the pathologically detrimental obsessive-compulsive tendencies that would've even made Howard Hughes stand back in amazement.

Like the "War on Terror" previously, the coronavirus codes-of-conduct have become the inescapable focus of our entire existence. It is the reason we are here, and we should devote our lives to ensure the Corona gods are happy. The "War Against Coronavirus" has become the new "War on Terror." Therefore, every action that we take must be predicated on the decisions of a handful of very powerful individuals (sociopaths really, most of whom you DIDN'T vote for) and their propaganda arm which is lovingly called, "The Free Press." For you must obey their edicts or face the literal or figurative boot of governmental power; used against folks they claim they are trying to "help," and ordered by power hungry politicians who aren't following any of the many "social distancing" orders and guidelines which they mandate us to follow. Odd, because you would think that if they, themselves, were worried about a deadly global virus which doesn't discriminate, then they'd WANT to do everything they are ordering you to do (under threat of violence, arrest, fines, and jail sentences). Not to mention, most of these individuals who you're obeying are the same folk I spoke of earlier: the ones who were tied to the most notorious and prolific human trafficker of the 21st century, Jeffrey Epstein.

Back in 2001, George W. Bush said matter-of-factly, "You're either with us, or you are with the terrorists." That same ultimatum has now been given

out by most governments of the world:
"You're either with us, or you are
with the virus."

My words are not meant to be
insensitive towards anyone suffering
from any illness. My words are not
meant to offend anyone. Do what you
feel you must in order to combat
illness. My only hope is that people
consider the implications of what all
of this means for humanity. If those
implications are not considered, you
may one day realize that you've lost
everything it means to be a human
being.

VI

JOURNAL ENTRY:
APRIL 15, 2020

Me: "What the government is doing is unconstitutional, authoritarian and totalitarian."

Others: "That's ridiculous. Go get fitted for a tinfoil hat."

Two. Days. Later.

Trump: "When somebody is the President of the United States, the authority is total."

Same Others: "That's unconstitutional and authoritarian! If Trump DOESN'T dictate that everyone be confined to their own house until 2022, indefinitely shut down all "nonessential business," and roll out mandatory covid vaccinations and immunity travel certificates... then he is literally Hitler."

Me: *facepalm*

VII

JOURNAL ENTRY:
APRIL 21, 2020

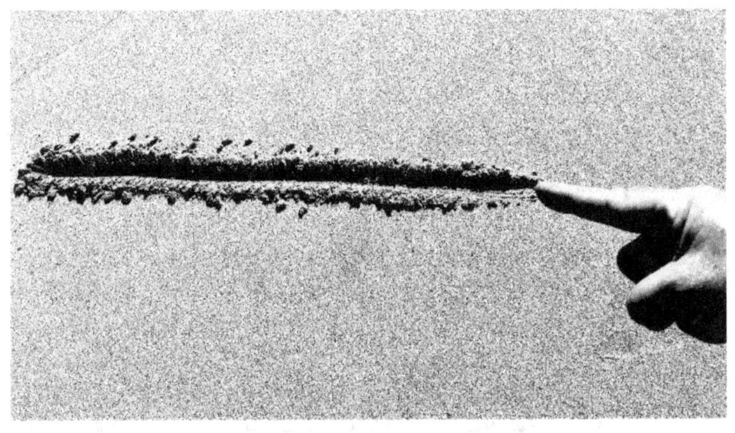

In regard to what governments order people to do, where do you all draw the line exactly? Since, obviously, the line ISN'T when they're shutting down the world economy, closing every small business, censoring differing opinions, introducing universal medical martial law (i.e. stay-at-home orders), not "allowing" people to make their own decisions regarding their own health, setting up police checkpoints to entrap "violators of executive orders," making nature walks or camping or fishing or surfing a "violation of social distancing orders," making it illegal to cross state lines unless you're an "essential worker," not allowing people to freely practice their religion in their place of worship, dishing out restraining orders to pastors for having church services, making protest illegal by stating that it violates the "congregation of 10 or above" orders (while simultaneously calling riots "mostly peaceful protests which should be encouraged"), dragging people off buses/putting them in choke holds/body slamming and arresting them for not wearing submission muzzels (er facemasks), conditioning children to be little robotic drones (who need to fear their fellow students, and to assume that everyone around them is a walking/talking bioweapon, and to not question anything coming out of the mouths of authority figures), urging people to snitch on their neighbors (Gestapo style), using smart devices to track people's every movement to see if they're following government edicts, rolling out vaccinations without the ability to sue manufacturers when they cause injury, certificates of immunization for participating in society (travel, work, banking, schooling, etc.), the WHO recommending that suspected Covid carriers be forcibly removed from their homes, Italy not medically treating anyone over 60 years old (setting the precedent for other countries if it came down to it), the Philippines shooting anyone who leaves their house (the US government has literally toppled foreign regimes for less. Iraq, Syria, Libya, etc., etc., etc.)...

Would the line be if the state mandated that you're only allowed to have one child, and any other pregnancy must be terminated? But don't worry, because it's to combat overpopulation and climate change. Is that where you'd draw the line? Or would you go along with that, too? You know, since the "experts" say so?

Would the line be if the state mandated a social crediting system?… where every action you take in life (since everything is tracked, tagged, and monitored) either raises or lowers your score, depending on whether the government approves of it or not; and the lower the score, the less privileges you have in society. But it's ok, because "official sources say" that it's the best way to produce a well behaved, well-mannered populace who does what they're told without question. By the way, if you think those previous two examples are over-exaggerated, they're not. That is how China already operates. And other countries' governments are looking to that as a blueprint for within their own borders.

Would the line be if the State mandated that every citizen be required to take an antidepressant (or any other drug, for that matter), if Bill Gates said it was for the best? Because, you know, people are just too damn sad all the time; and they need to forget about all the bad stuff in the world that causes negative feelings… like war, orchestrated food shortages, lack of access to resources, social isolation, not being able to see family, not being able to make a living, not being able to pay bills, not being able to provide for your children, not being able to leave your house, etc.

All that stuff just needs to be buried in the pit of your stomach with FDA approved psychotropics; rather than people getting sun, exercising, having access to healthy food options and buying vegetable seeds to make a garden, or God forbid, seeing family or having a social support system. Those things are nonessential activities, and unnecessary for a fulfilling and soul-enriching human experience. All a person really needs to be healthy is Pop Tarts, Walmart, Netflix, and mainstream news to live a happy, healthy life. The rest is just fluff, anyway. In fact, if you engage in anything else, you are a selfish, entitled, narcissistic, Hitler-like "a-hole" who wants grandparents to die. *sarcasm* How dare you petition the government for a redress of grievances, you entitled jerks. You're acting like you have inalienable rights as a human being, which can't be taken away (the nerve!). What do you think?.. that this is a free country or something? You know that the purpose of your life is to understand that the government's needs are paramount to all else.Anyone who says differently is an unscientific, conspiracy theorist nutjob.

Anywho, as I asked in the beginning… where do you all draw the line, exactly?

VIII

JOURNAL ENTRY:
May 1, 2020

The past few months have been a
strange time. I've watched people
freak out over a lack of toilet paper,
as though it is some life-sustaining

substance. I've watched individuals who'd, in the past, had rightly justified concerns about Hispanic migrants being locked up in detention centers (saying it's a human rights violation) suddenly praising authorities for placing the whole country on house arrest without due process; supporting and encouraging the arrest, detainment, and solitary confinement of those who don't strictly adhere to the arbitrary social distancing guideline edicts (which governments keep making up out of thin air, each and every day.. while the authorities adhere to none of them); expressing their wish and hope that those who voice their concerns by means of organizing constitutionally protected gatherings/assemblies/services/protests will contract, suffer from, and/or die from the virus... a virus that everyone must base the rest of their lives on and accommodate... so that they may learn the errors of their wrong-think, and fall in line with hivemind orthodoxy.

I've watched people in grocery and sporting goods stores unquestioningly following arrows and standing six feet apart at their designated duct tape "X"...as though every six feet is its own parallel universe, with its own air supply... and not 5 feet 11 inches by God... it has to be six feet EXACTLY, otherwise the magical force field doesn't work. I've seen people driving in cars by themselves with the whole "facemask and glove" combo, genuinely believing that they're protected from airborne pathogens. I've even seen people posting social media family photos in which everyone is wearing said facemasks.

Long story short... when I'm anywhere out and about in this "New Normal" World Order... I feel like this is how Tom Cruise's character in "Eyes Wide Shut" must've felt when he accidentally stumbled into the Illuminati Initiation ritual. Definitely a, "What in the ever-loving fuck is all this shit?," kind of a time we are currently going through.

IX

JOURNAL ENTRY:

May 9, 2020

Fact Checkers Misleading
Misinformation News Media Political
Truth DISINFORMATION
Social Media Alternative Facts
Spread The Left Fake News
Lies Conspiracy Theories Lawsuits
Defamation Deceive Big Tech
Public Opinion False The Right

I find it interesting how quickly people are to condemn, ridicule, guilt trip, freak out over, and go out of their way to purge from social media any information and/or individuals who express differing viewpoints.. justifying its removal by labeling it (what they consider to be) "harmful misinformation"...and then acting as though national and mainstream news sources are the ones producing "facts" and "trustworthy" information which cannot be questioned.

I watched the mini-doc "Plandemic," and it was actually pretty tame and brief as far as "rabbit hole conspiracy theories" go. It's not the first time this current situation has been called "plandemic," either. They didn't come up with that expression. Many independent investigators and/or journalists have called it "plandemic" or "scamdemic" for as long as this has been going on. And, no, (for the millionth time) I'm not saying the virus is fake. But to pretend that somehow Bill Gates is undoubtedly the voice of reason in this situation (as if he doesn't have his own financial/personal/global/societal aspirations for what he's promoting), or pretending that Anthony Fauci is free from all political/financial/medical coercion... while simultaneously stating that this Dr. Judy Mikovits is pure evil, spouting antivax propaganda and spewing nonsensical conspiracy theories.. because she's allegedly an "attention-seeking nutjob" who holds a grudge and "has a score to settle".. is mere cognitive dissonance, if nothing else. She, specifically, and unlike Gates and Fauci, has an agenda... and she MUST be stopped. *sarcasm*

I don't really care who she is, but that doesn't take away from her point that Bill Gates and Anthony Fauci aren't exactly the most trustworthy of people. And again, none of these authorities or experts whom you're taking pecking orders from are engaging in the "life saving" social distancing protocols... while they shame anyone else who doesn't abide by them. Fauci, Cuomo, Gates, Pritzker, Redfield, Obama, Trump, the W.H.O... none of them are abiding by their own restrictions. None of them.

It's not like Mikovits is the only person to have raised concerns over what's taking place. Many medical professionals have raised concerns on social media, only to be banned from the platforms each and every time. Because having ideas is a scary thing, and that must be eradicated in order to protect people from sorting things out on their own. *sarcasm* People are acting like the government has never gone out of their way to try to destroy people's reputations or unjustly imprisoned folks for speaking out against immoral actions and policies, systematically carried out through government edict. Martin Luther King, Jr. and Malcolm X are perfect examples. More modern examples are as follows...

Edward Snowden was a former NSA employee turned whistleblower who exposed the government's mass surveillance programs, at a time before it was admitted by government to be the case, and before people had grown accustomed and complacent to the notion that there is literally no privacy in anyone's life (when it comes to what the government has access to). For his trouble, now Snowden must live in exile for the rest of his days or risk getting arrested and put in prison for exposing these illegal and unconstitutional actions of the government.

Julian Assange exposed U.S. Government war crimes and other governmental corruption through Wikileaks, and what kind of thanks does he get? He's been rotting in jail, and his health is deteriorating.

These gentlemen used to be champions of the political left... used to be, when it was politically convenient for them to be. Now in our New Corona World Order.. the elimination of privacy, the elimination of personal autonomy, obscenely blatant government overreach, and setting fire to the constitution is not only "necessary," but demanded into existence by people, in order to "combat the covid." Folks are defending these government actions as fervently as other people defended the toppling of Libya in 2011, or the "weapons of mass destruction" lie back in 2003, or the Patriot Act drafted after 9/11, or the government's role in the Waco Massacre in 1993, or our government's backing of the mujahideen in the early 80's, or Richard Nixon prior to Watergate in the early 70's, or the Gulf of Tonkin Resolution in

1964 (psst, the Gulf of Tonkin incident was falsified in order to justify the Vietnam War), etc., etc., etc..

None of the examples above are conjecture or, as people like to label it, "conspiracy theory." They are all incidents in which the government lied, manipulated, used, killed, massacred, committed genocide, and/or left entire generations of people devastated, desolate, and dead... all in the name of "keeping people safe." And there are many, many more examples. Those are just the ones I thought of off the top of my head. There's a good reason why people should be extremely skeptical when government figures, media pundits, and yes, even government-appointed doctors and "experts" start preaching to people about "safety" and "security." It has nothing to do with "gullible people" buying into "conspiratorial nonsense," and everything to do with people recognizing that governments lie, cheat, steal, and murder to get what they want. They don't care about you. They don't care about your family. They don't care if you get sick. They don't care if you die. They (the governments) spend their free time figuring out ways to bomb the fuck out of third world countries (killing millions in the process), or how to turn stable regions into unstable, desperate cesspools giving rise to each and every new terrorist group, hell bent on retribution; thereby giving government an excuse to intervene in the regions' affairs till the end of time. Do you really think they give a damn if you get a virus?

All of the aforementioned events or situations were unquestioningly supported by national and mainstream media outlets. In most cases, they do not acknowledge or apologize for promoting and parroting humanity-crushing misinformation... harmful lies that have led to the deaths, displacement, and degradation of countless millions of people. But, yeah.. a 26 minute long "conspiracy" video, I tell you, that's a dangerous matter of life and death. *sarcasm*

Modern liberals have been duped into supporting censorship, police brutality, preemptive universal detainment, closing borders (state by state), banning protests, government dictating what you can and can't do with your own body, the elimination of the working class, surveillance state spying, and snitching on your neighbor... as long as it keeps you safe from coronavirus.

But yeah, those people who shared "Plandemic" on Facebook... they're the naive ones. Right. *eyeroll* At least those "conspiracy" folks don't spend their time trolling other people's posts, trying to tell you what you have to think on matters, or just repeating CNN and Snopes talking points.

X

JOURNAL ENTRY:
May 30, 2020

As far as those riots that plagued the nation go: you're all still being manipulated with them. You're being played like a fiddle. People are responding on cue to exactly how the government wants them to respond. It all leads to more restrictions for us, and more power for the State. The government is most likely trying to trigger a civil war with all of the violence and destruction.

Everything that happens in this country is turned into a left vs. right situation to keep us fighting with each other. Scapegoats are occasionally thrown to the wolves(like the cop who was charged, or like when Epstein was jailed and subsequently "killed himself") to make people feel as though something has been done.

Peaceful, nonviolent civil disobedience is being phased out by means of the system's equating it with violent riots. They call all riots that break out in this country "protests," thereby de-legitimizing any justifiable grievance that ordinary citizens may have. For some reason, twisting language to suit their own Orwellian objectives has been extremely effective at stamping out true opposition to State corruption.

The business of waging war, while keeping the nation in a docile slumber, has been ingeniously implemented for decades now. This is done by making us believe that if we just vote the correct people into office, then things will finally improve. They've left nothing to chance in these Reality-TV political playoffs, which the people invest so much time, energy, and money into supporting. Those in power are going to do what they do regardless of how much campaigning people do for any candidate.

The truth of the matter is that we can change all of those things right now simply by refusing to comply with any corrupt, unjust, or immoral action which the government orders its people to obey. But for that, there needs to be people willing to do it; and there isn't. The system is set up to keep people too busy, distracted, and dependent on that system to actually stand up to it. You don't need violent actions to change things. Non-compliance is what will change things. It's literally impossible for a handful of "authority figures" to control 300 million Americans unless we acquiesce to their directives.

With this in mind, remember that "protests" of any kind (peaceful, mostly peaceful, or not peaceful at all) don't really work when it comes down to it. That is because the ruling class doesn't recognize the rights of ordinary people in the first place. Protesting is only effective when a governing body recognizes and respects people as human beings. Begging tyrants to govern us more nicely only serves to make the ruling class laugh in our faces. If the citizenry refused to pay taxes (on the other hand), that is an instantaneous, tangible, and effective means of showing the rulers that we're not gonna take their crap anymore. Not only is this a nonviolent approach, but it also makes it unnecessary to put the ordinary citizens who have grievances in harm's way. The only problem with this is that mass numbers of people have to be on board with it, in order for it to be effective. But that's the way to do it.

XI

JOURNAL ENTRY:
JUNE 10, 2020

The thought of the institution of police being a thing of the past has been kind of a pipe dream of mine for several years, and for multiple reasons. Libertarians have suggested ways of lessening the government's abilities to abuse their power for decades, including restricting government branches' authorities, as well as law enforcement authorities. Libertarians have wanted an end to No Knock Raids, an end to victimless drug laws, an end to illegal wars of aggression, etc. Doing away with funding the very institutions which limit our abilities to live as free and unimpeded individuals isn't a new argument which sprang into existence with the death of George Floyd. It has been a staple of Libertarian philosophy, for as long as the term has been around. So it's interesting to see an across-the-board embracing of such ideas, when they've been met with ridicule for so long, even at the mere suggestion of such concepts.

Good general rule of thumb... if government and media figure heads are jumping on the bandwagon and embracing an idea which they've spent their entire careers scorning and writing off as "ridiculous" and "not feasible," it's probably a safe bet that they're not doing it out of the goodness of their hearts. But you can bet your ass that they will be using this situation and momentum to push through their own objectives which they've been holding onto, for just such an occasion (and for just the right public support) while making everyone think that it was the public's idea in the first place. You sometimes need to be careful that you don't get steamrolled, yourself, in the process of what you're getting behind.

That being said... If you, now, as a government or media figurehead, support the defunding and dismantling of police departments, then who's gonna enforce your precious Executive

Stay-at-Home Orders and Social Engineering (I mean, "Distancing") Guidelines which you've been espousing as practically necessary for the continuation of the species this year? I mean, before you started embracing the idea that it's apparently ok to risk killing the elderly with covid as long as there's a really good social-justice reason; conveniently forgetting that your main talking point for keeping people in line during the lockdowns was, "You don't care about the elderly and immunocompromised if you don't follow social distancing orders."

Now, even George W. Bush, himself, has become a champion of civil rights and has "taken a stand against racism." Guys, George W. Bush INVENTED racism (I'm speaking hyperbolically, not literally, but you get my point.. since some don't understand the concept of satire/sarcasm). Do you all not remember what his administration's response to New Orleans was after Hurricane Katrina? They were basically like, "Eh, fuck 'em. They're on their own.".. and the authorities forcibly confiscated the residents' firearms, meaning they could no longer protect themselves, 'cause why not? Oh yeah, and that's beside the fact that Bush started wars against, imprisoned, and tortured folks who had nothing to do with 9/11 while implementing cutesy Orwellian legislation like "The Patrio Act" and "Enhanced

Interrogation." All of which paved the way for the very governmental and law enforcement abuses which are being carried out to this very day, because he "cares very deeply about civil rights." Yeah, right.

All I'm saying is to be careful that you're not being handed the shackles which you're trying to remove.

XII

JOURNAL ENTRY: JUNE 28, 2020

This is an overview of one of my favorite movies, and how it relates to the current world in which we live. *spoiler alerts*

Despite the fact that "V for Vendetta" represents a revolutionary's wet dream scenario for overthrowing a despotic government, I would encourage everyone to go back and rewatch this film, and try to understand the concepts it was expressing.

In the film, the character "V" had been an unwilling test subject for his government's "Nazi-like" biological weapons research program, which resulted in mass genocide of civilians. After escaping from the facility, and spending years in hiding, he took on the persona of a "Guy Fawkes Masked Vigilante and Revolutionary."

As this new persona, he dismantled the corrupt criminal courts which didn't live up to their own promise of a balance of justice (nor did they maintain fairness and equality, nor prevent anyone in power from getting away with atrocities). He dismantled the corrupt state-run media, which peddled and perpetuated government propaganda; lies which lulled the citizenry into a state of subservience, in every manner. He dismantled the corrupt and illegitimate government itself, which had become an authoritarian fascist entity with no regard for human life, nor societal freedoms. And he went after the very individuals who were personally responsible for ordering, taking part in, or allowing crimes against humanity to be committed; those who, therefore, were getting away with those crimes... because of the corrupt courts, media, and the illegitimate government.

Conversely, these are some of the things he didn't do. The character "V" didn't burn down fast food chains or department stores like Wendy's,

Target, or AutoZone. He didn't change the brand names of syrup and desserts. He didn't take certain content out of cartoons. He didn't try to silence comedians/entertainers because they made a joke or because they laughed at the wrong joke. He didn't shadow ban independent journalists from expressing and publishing their non-corporate funded views and research. He didn't turn ordinary citizens against each other. Also, he didn't instruct ordinary people to blindly obey government doctrine for the illusion of safety and security. In fact, the only thing V encouraged the people to do was to NOT comply with the authoritarian government. In other words, he went after the heart of the matter of the injustices, rather than going after situations and symptoms.. nor did he broad brush entire groups of everyday individuals and/or institutions which ultimately had nothing to do with the bigger problem at hand.

While the film, itself, represents a metaphorical "worst case scenario" for how terrible an unchecked power can be, the manner in which real life governments have been able to condition their populations into reacting and responding in ways which only serve to benefit the State, at the expense of everyone else (not to mention the systems of smart surveillance and the loss of personal autonomy, liberty, and destiny) is not too awfully far off from how the film portrayed society.

However, though, it isn't even necessary to engage in any destructive act, which only gives governments a greater excuse to tighten restrictions over everyone (to, as they call it, "restore order"). Because, guess what? They're still siphoning money out of your wallet to do those things. In effect, you are paying these governments to beat the crap out of you, or worse. Do you really think they give a damn if you're asking them to treat you kinder?

Noncompliance is how you stop corrupt governments. If you think those in power are behaving in ways that are detrimental to the physical, emotional, financial, and political wellbeing of everyone involved, then stop funding them (in mass). Stop paying them to beat your ass or anyone else's, figuratively and literally. They need you a lot more than you need them. And once they can't control you (by taking your own money from you) then their jig is up.

In the 60's, the hippie liberal motto was, "Give Peace a Chance." That seems to have been replaced by the modern liberal motto of, "Give Destruction a Chance." We have the equivalent of a "Schrodinger's Protestor" where we should simultaneously recognize any acts of rioting as a genuine, legitimate, and healthy means of expression for marginalized groups who feel as though they have no voice in society; and at the same time we should recognize that these acts don't represent the message of the protests: as they are apparently carried out by "provocateurs who infiltrated the groups, and don't represent the movement." None of the above even has to transpire when people are a united front who won't comply with unchecked power. Peace is noncompliance. Noncompliance is revolution. It's the most fundamental of checks and balances. This is what the film "V for Vendetta" is really all about.

Don't allow yourself to be blinded into hate. Don't waste your energy on despising your neighbor. Anyone's personal preferences of political puppets, and your personal disdain for those puppets (and the people who support them) isn't going to make a lick of difference when the government uses that momentum against you, and against others.

"Hate cannot drive out hate; only love can do that." - Martin Luther King, Jr.

XIII

JOURNAL ENTRY:
AUGUST 9, 2020

Event 201 was a tabletop pandemic exercise that took place on October 18, 2019 in New York City... and brought to you by the World Economic Forum, the Bill and Melinda Gates Foundation, and John Hopkins University. This was a month or two before covid 19 was even known to exist. The exercise dealt with a"novel coronavirus" which was transmitted "from bats to pigs to people" and spread globally.

If world governments' preparedness and readiness for a novel coronavirus was such that they were able to have a global pandemic exercise scenario for the very situation that came about in real life a few months later (except that the fictional exercise virus was far more deadly), then one needs to ask themselves WHY it is that responses were botched in such a way that the entire planet was turned upside down into a state of cataclysmic, catastrophic, and devastating turmoil/hardship; where human beings aren't even allowed to make the most basic decisions over their own lives.. You know? Since the authorities and experts envisioned these very scenarios playing themselves out, took into account the majority of troubleshooting happenstances, determined what was "essential vs. nonessential", established hypothetical travel bans and restrictions, expected foreseeable economic fallout, anticipated crumbling supply chains, used phrases like "the new normal," described rioting in the streets, and made an artistic rendition of the fictitious novel coronavirus which looks very similar to what we all recognize as covid 19; since they had enough time, energy, effort, and funding to create worldwide cooperation from many governments and organizations, and even took the time to make mock news stories and updates from their fictional GNN news channel… whose reports and talking points (at least the words within) were virtually indistinguishable from what we see going on in the world today.

This exercise, which John Hopkins University and the Bill and Melinda Gates foundation were involved in, isn't a "conspiracy theory." It's in recent historical record, and coming from their own mouths: the mouths of those who are currently (as we speak) shaping policies for life in the "New Normal" world order.

XIV

JOURNAL ENTRY:
AUGUST 15, 2020

Public service announcement for those who've wrongly assumed that social media platforms are for you to discuss, engage, promote, and exchange concepts, ideas, and philosophies in a free and open format, for the purpose of bringing every one of us closer together; especially in times when we're supposed to minimize (or even completely do away with) all forms of in-person social interactions (unless specifically pre-approved or sanctioned by the State and/or your lovable governors and local authorities). You poor, poor, misinformed, freethinking, disillusioned, Constitution-quoting idealists. As if the Constitution even applies to anything anymore [enter condescending, maniacal laughter here].

Looks like someone's gonna have to remind you radical freedom-lovers which subjects are off limits in regards to your own personal thoughts, inquires, and musings; while I say it in a stern, parental, finger-pointing, patronizing tone in order to make sure you know how serious these demands and instructions are for conversing with friends or acquaintances on your own personal social media page.

1) You can't talk about or even be troubled by human-trafficking unless it's trafficking that the content-checking, censoring, keyboard gatekeepers say you can talk about.

2) You cannot talk about government crimes, corruption, mistakes, mishandlings, or nefarious intentions ever; because the government is infallible, they have never lied, and they are never wrong. Everything they say is only to ensure that the health and security of you, your family, and everyone you personally know are always the number one top priority, and you are a conspiracy nut if you think otherwise; unless you're talking about Russian bots or literally anything to do with Trump… as he is solely responsible for everything that

has gone wrong in this country for the last four years (and I do mean EVERYTHING), along with anyone wearing a red cap.

3) You also can't question anything that comes out the mouths of the self-appointed experts, as they are also godlike in their infallibility; even (and especially) when they do a 180° every other day in regards to telling you how you must live and behave, every moment of your life. Unless, of course, those experts disagree with OUR experts, or if they have the wrong political affiliation; then, you can't believe those propagandists, because those jerks are just right-wing extremists who want to usher in the Fourth Reich. Therefore, there's no reason to listen to anything they say… EVER (even if they're not right leaning, nor conservative, nor Republican… 'cause that's just perfect cover. Those folks who've never spent a day in their lives having anything to do with conservatism and, in fact, have spent all that time trying to encourage everyone to live together peacefully and to do no harm; those fake hippies are the perfect recruits for white nationalism, and don't let them tell you any different. Those peace-loving, anti-violence, antiwar, anti-police-brutality, conspiracy nuts who've been warning people about the abuses of government power since before you were born, they are sooooo out of touch; and their advocacy of

personal autonomy and civil liberties are really just euphemisms and microaggressions for justifying racism, misogyny, and patriarchal oppression.

4) You can't bring up any historical or modern examples/instances of government engaging in blatantly unethical experimentation, incarceration, or extermination against civilians of this country or others (and gotten away with it scot-free), because that never happened, EVER. Stupid conspiracy theorists. Smh.

5) Oh, and you're only allowed to be heartbroken, devastated, and concerned about the tragic murders against the innocent and undeserving individuals when we, the gatekeepers, say you can be outraged by it. Every death must be polarized except for the type mentioned in the previous bullet point; which we'll gladly ignore, overlook, and explain away as "crackpot theories." We, the keyboard gatekeepers, get to tell you how you're supposed to feel about each and every one that happens, unless it's on a day when our self-righteousness isn't fully charged. Then, it can be (and will be) ignored as well, unless someone has the audacity to bring attention to it.

Oh yeah, and this is satire, in case any of that went over anyone's head,

and only establishment-approved
satire is permitted on your social
media platforms in this year of
"1984."

XV

JOURNAL ENTRY: SEPTEMBER 11, 2020

In the aftermath of 9/11, the EPA stated publicly that the air quality was "safe to breathe." Therefore, they claimed that the first responders, the volunteers, and local residents didn't need the proper equipment to shield their lungs from breathing in the extremely toxic sludge that was the air at Ground Zero. As a result of the government's negligent medical advice, people from that area have and will continue to get sick and die from serious lung issues related to 9/11. These folks selflessly worked around the clock to dig through debris, or to try to help in any other way they could. These individuals, including the families of those who have already died off, still have to fight on a regular basis just to be compensated for all of the endless piles of medical bills that they've accumulated as thanks for their selfless acts.

The above examples should scream out to people today, beyond a shadow of a doubt, that when government agencies and politicians come out of the woodwork to remind you how seriously they take the safety, health, and general well-being of their citizens when making their decisions about how you all can operate your lives during these most difficult of days; you can rest assured (and without reservation) that they are LYING.

And that's aside from the criminal governmental negligence at every level that resulted in the 9/11 events themselves, but I'll save that rant for another time.

XVI

JOURNAL ENTRY:
OCTOBER 15, 2020

According to CNBC, total billionaire wealth has skyrocketed to a "record high" of $10.2 trillion during the Covid crisis. So, the biggest wealth transfer in human history goes to the same individuals and/or companies who declared themselves "essential" while preaching the necessity of limiting, stifling, restricting, or closing any business deemed "non essential," for the "safety and security" of mankind.

These multi-billionaires are the ones who also support, promote, lobby, and pave the way for every single one of the "new normals" which ordinary people around the globe are expected to follow, in order to participate in society. Meanwhile, the people on the lowest rungs of the socioeconomic ladder support and defend these very same positions put in place by the billionaires they say they hate. Long story short: in order for the "1%" to maintain power and control, they had to rebrand themselves as supporters of the other 99%.

As an outside observer of partisan politics, it appears as though the citizens who buy into mainstream political paradigms are being manipulated into demanding that "their way" (by which I mean, the restrictions and behaviors they've been convinced are best for the rest of humanity) be forced onto others, regardless of personal convictions.

In that paradigm, if total lockdowns are used as a response to inhabitants allegedly not taking extra precautions, then those lockdowns are viewed as no longer an excessive abridgment of an individual's rights, and are therefore justified. The same line of thinking is used to justify all the varying degrees of draconian measures which governments all over the world have implemented during this pandemic, while passing it off as unquestionable and extinction-preventing "science."

My question is: "What exactly is the scientific difference between an alleged nonessential, non-state sanctioned gathering of 20 or 30 people (or however many) for any reason; be it a BBQ, a church service, a funeral, a protest (mostly peaceful, peaceful, or not peaceful at all); and an alleged "essential" activity like the 10,000 people per day or so who go into a Walmart?"

They're touching all the same items everyone else touched, using the same touchscreens everyone else uses for financial transactions, putting those potential super-spreader items into one's car, taking off one's mask after handling all those items, and taking them home without thoroughly bleaching each and every one. But that's an "essential" activity, so that stops germs dead in their tracks, I guess?

Modern liberals are partaking in alleged "risky and reckless gatherings," same as modern conservatives. The "liberals" just aren't demonized for it. They're having the same family gatherings, parties, and/or protests (mostly peaceful or otherwise), but they still get virtue-signaling points for criticizing anyone else who gets together for any reason. Despite the fact that practically every business has implemented mask mandates for its customers, the virus spreads regardless. And when it does, again, only certain people are blamed for the spread when practically everyone is engaging in the same behavior to some degree or another.

Meanwhile, governors like Andrew Cuomo (who's been praised for his lockdown measures) placed Covid-positive elderly patients into nursing homes, causing the further spread and deaths of very vulnerable individuals. Not only that, but his brother, Chris Cuomo, is the news anchor who has preached and virtue-signaled on a daily basis about the absolute and inarguable necessity of wearing facemasks in any and every public setting; while Andrew imposed the facemask mandates for New York.

Well, according to the New York Post, Chris' apartment management sent him a letter of notification for his continuous refusal to wear a mask at times when it is required to do so, and told him that they will fine him if they have to. Both Chris and Andrew Cuomo have spent the past several months basically stating that refusal to wear masks is tantamount to manslaughter. Cuomo wouldn't wear a mask, and he also broke quarantine back when he was diagnosed with Covid (several months ago). Yet, anyone else who doesn't do what these two men say is "evil" …according to them. The hypocrisy is mind-numbing.

Your news anchors are full of it. Your politicians are full of it. The billionaires who buy them are full of it. They don't care about your health, safety, and standards of living. They simply get a rush from telling you what you must do, under threat of governmental punishment (while ignoring their own rules). But it's ok, because they won't be called out on it, and they'll still get to keep their lucrative jobs at the end of the day; all while their listeners are living and dying through a new Great Depression. But, we're all supposed to follow what these "leaders" and their "experts" say to do.

I'm simply implying that everything put in place to allegedly prevent, halt, or slow the spread hasn't done anything except cause more problems, more illnesses, more hunger, more poverty, more mental health issues, more suicides, more hatred between ordinary citizens, and more dependence on those institutions. Institutions, which ultimately don't really care if people live or die from any illness or economic hardship… as those politicians, pundits, institutions, and billionaires can use it all for political benefit and leverage, when it's all said and done.

Good rule of thumb: don't base your entire existence on the whims of ultra-powerful elites who never abide by their own rules. Their "recommendations" are the cause of these hardships, not the remedy. They have made the majority of people's lives more increasingly difficult to navigate, with each and every update of the "settled science." Be cautious and be vigilant, for it's easy to fall prey to these life-altering societal paradigms. And while they may claim altruistic motives, the money flow seems to indicate that it only benefits the few, at the expense of the many.

XVII

JOURNAL ENTRY:
DECEMBER 5, 2020

Remember everyone, you must listen to and obey your elected officials and the experts. You must cancel everything. And I mean EVERYTHING. That includes Christmas, you selfish bastids. Exchanging and unwrapping presents from loved ones, going to Christmas mass, and enjoying a family feast are all super spreader events. If you engage in anything remotely similar to that, it'll be your "last supper." It's no longer PC enough to just say "happy holidays." Now you must cancel and forsake any and all holidays, unless you want Jolly Old St. Nick to leave the plague under everyone's tree. And no, you naysayers, this isn't a War on Christmas... It's the War on Covid. And you must sacrifice everything to appease the will of your new lord and savior, Anthony Fauci.

And always remember... your sacrifices make it possible, everyday, for your elected officials and experts to have more leg room while they're deep throating turkey legs and guzzling $15,000 of wine (in one sitting) at their own private dinners, celebrations, and gatherings... while reminding you to make a $1,200 slave check stretch for 9 months, as your local businesses are flushed down the toilet.

And if you're lucky, they'll even wave another $1000 check in your face, if you'll swear a blood oath... I mean... roll up your sleeve and take the 100% safe and effective (and totally not rushed) vaccine, which has zero side effects and totally isn't exempted from legal liability if you happen to be damaged from it in some way. That's just Russian disinformation.

Because the government, especially YOUR government, is in the business of giving you things for free (and even paying you) with absolutely no strings attached. They just care about you, your safety, your health, and your

well-being that friggin much
people. C'mon man, gotta give 'em
props for that.

Let us pray...

Our Fauci..
Who art in Washington..
Hallowed be thy guidelines.

Thy tyranny come..
Thy will be done..
In our own homes, as it is in WalMart.
Give us this day our daily lockdowns..
And forgive us our trespasses..
As we NEVER forgive those who don't
wear a mask..
And lead us not into human
interaction..
But deliver us from covid. Amen and
Awomen.

XVIII

JOURNAL ENTRY:
JANUARY 7, 2021

Anti-establishment in the 90's: "Fuck you, I won't do what you tell me!"

Anti-establishment in 2021: "Fuck you, DO WHAT WE TELL YOU!"

It's also adorable that people really think that all it takes to "storm" the most heavily secured areas, locations, and buildings in the country is just to have quote unquote "rednecks" walk up with Trump flags and horns on their head, all while posing for high def publicity photos, while managing to scale two-dozen-foot tall walls. That is what amounts to a "coup d'etat?"

So, I guess on 9/11, all that Al Qaeda would've needed to do was walk right in to Washington buildings and declare themselves the new rulers? That's all it takes? They didn't even need to go about having their amateur Cessna pilots elaborately hijack four commercial jumbo jetliners (which they managed to pull off with box cutters), penetrate the most restricted airspace on planet earth, perfectly fly and crash them into strategic financial and political targets (even though they'd never set foot inside the cockpit of a 767 before that day) while the most expensive defense agencies and rulers of the free world sat on their asses until the majority of the death and destruction had already taken place? They could've just saved themselves all that trouble and just walked right in with Trump flags, and the most powerful empire on planet earth would've scattered like frightened chihuahuas, and merely politely escorted themselves out of the chambers? Then the 19 would-be hijackers could've simply declared Osama Bin Laden to be the new president? Seems legit.

I suppose the age of innocence has not yet left this land, and is still captivating full grown adults who long to believe in televised governmental public relations fairytales. It's encouraging, really.

XIX

JOURNAL ENTRY:

JANUARY 13, 2021

Back in February of 2003, Colin Powell
appeared before the UN to make his
administration's case for preemptive
military intervention against Iraq.
His entire presentation (based on b.s.
"intelligence") was loaded with
fabricated claims that Iraq was hiding
weapons of mass destruction, that they
were tied to Al Qaeda (and therefore
allegedly complicit in the 9/11
attacks), and that they were refusing
to disarm; complete with computer

generated cartoon imagery of apparent "mobile bioweapons production facilities," and satellite imagery of random buildings which they circled and erroneously labeled "explosives factories." He even held up a model vial of "anthrax" while making his case for war. Powell went so far as to say, "These are not assertions. What we are giving you are facts and conclusions based on solid intelligence."

Now, aside from the fact that the Bush, Jr. administration had already made up its mind that they were going to invade Iraq by the time Powell gave his UN presentation, and aside from the fact that preemptive wars of aggression are international crimes against humanity (laid out plain as day during the Nuremberg Trials, post WW2), this was a very blatant instance of top U.S. government officials inciting the toppling (or the "overthrow," if you will) of a sovereign nation based entirely on conjecture and conspiracy theory (in the truest sense of the word THEORY).

Because of this (oh, how do you say it) spreading of harmful misinformation, around 200,000 innocent civilians were killed in Iraq, 4,424 U.S. soldiers were killed in Iraq, and 31,952 U.S. soldiers were wounded in action in Iraq. And that's just Iraq. That doesn't include civilian and military deaths/wounded from the six other countries the U.S. Government decided to invade/carpet bomb during their 20-year-long (so far) "War on Terror."

These events were brought into existence by a group of reactionary statists known as the Neoconservatives: Bush, Cheney, Wolfowitz, Rumsfeld, Tenet, Kristol, etc. The operations were championed by the majority of Democrats of the time, as well, including a gentleman by the name of Joe Biden. You might've heard of him. As he, along with the majority of the Democrat establishment are just as responsible (and just as guilty) of these egregious crimes against humanity as those Neoconservative elites were/are. Yet all of these individuals are now, generally, viewed in a positive light, are considered to be respectful statesmen, and are often praised for their most important commonality... allegedly being "opposed" to Trump. Now... I personally believe that Trump is a war criminal, as well; and for the same reasons I believe that Bush, Cheney, Obama, and Clinton are. However, everyone of those other establishment politicians are NOT banned from any and all social media platforms, nor was there any attempts to impeach anyone else for the demonstrable war crimes which took place (not to mention the hundreds of thousands, if not millions, of civilians killed because of their decisions, i.e. "incitements").

Now, I don't want them to be banned from speaking on platforms either. However, my point in all of this is simply that those prominent figures in politics and media who are so completely and utterly indignant over the "evils" of the current ceremonial figurehead we call the "POTUS," and others who may fixate and parrot similar indignation at the mere mention of the POS's name... I mean, POTUS's name... are either disingenuous, selective in their outrage, or completely blinded by pure hatred of a reality tv star whom they were conditioned to focus all of their energy on.

Even comedians or personalities whom I used to admire quite a bit, such as Stephen Colbert, seem to have adopted this mentality. Early in his career, he had the balls to go to the White House Correspondents dinner and perform a heavy-hitting 25-minute televised satirical indictment of Bush as a war criminal while sitting just 10 feet away from him (at a time when most Americans still supported Bush and his actions). But now, Colbert has seemed to be one of those infected with Trump Derangement Syndrome, and pushes the manipulative false narrative that half the population within this country are a bunch of enablers at best, and extremist insurrectionists at worst.

From what I see, all of this vindictiveness and attempts to silence/purge differing viewpoints, doesn't have a lot to do with love, tolerance, acceptance, nor a wish to help improve the conditions for the human race; especially when one considers that none of that energy was spent on trying to prevent, minimize, or put a stop to the millions of civilian deaths caused by U.S. government foreign policy in the Middle East. That kind of thing isn't just police brutality; it's World Police Brutality. But I guess Iraqi lives don't matter to the arbiters of "righteous" indignation.

Now, again, this is all coming from someone who doesn't even like Trump; not as a person, nor as a reality tv star, nor as a politician. I have no stake in the matter of whether or not he's in office, because I think that he's just as corrupt as all the others I've mentioned in this writing. But take a step back and actually analyze the types of measures that you may be currently applauding; whether it's the support for the banning of certain individuals from social media, or jumping on the bandwagon of demonizing anyone who doesn't exactly share (or fit into) your current particular political ideology (based on manipulated, skewed, and false narratives which inundate and bombard the airwaves from every direction on a daily basis). And when it comes down to it, that type of bullying into compliance or silence won't just be used against those you happen to vehemently disagree with. It will eventually be used to silence your voice as well.

As the opening segment of this writing pointed out, these kinds of perceptual manipulations can be used to justify more than just the censorship of unpopular opinions. It can be used to justify unspeakable crimes against humanity, and this is what governments are in the business of. That is why they spend so much time fomenting division. Kindness, compassion, empathetic listening, and peaceful interactions, on the other hand, are a good way to counter and even overcome society's tendency to want to polarize everything in sight. In these tumultuous times, it's more important than ever to set aside petty differences and to be a beacon of reason and positivity to those around you.

XX

JOURNAL ENTRY:
JANUARY 19, 2021

Leading up to the inauguration, several members of the Army National Guard were removed from inauguration duty because of alleged inappropriate comments/texts, or alleged questionable associations. So, they're good enough to be sent overseas to fight against peasant sheep herders in the Middle East for the "War on Terror," but they're not good enough for inauguration duty because they might not have the correct political views; and thereby, "might" be a "threat" to the incoming administration? In other words, they're not being vetted and background checked to prove loyalty to the country; but rather, they're being screened to prove loyalty to Biden?

Does anyone remember a time when, after 9/11, society was being conditioned to view anyone with an Islamic sounding name with suspicion, because they might somehow be "associated" or "sympathetic" to Islamic extremists or Al Qaeda?.. even though that line of reasoning and logic is completely and utterly unwarranted, unjustified, unamerican, prejudice, and actually racist?

Well, they're using that exact same playbook to use against a different demographic here at home for the purpose of stirring tension, hostility, paranoia, and distrust towards the 75 million Americans who voted for a certain political figure, or the millions of others who aren't strictly loyal to another incoming puppet.

I'm kinda surprised this needs to be explained in 2021, but blaming entire groups of people for the actions of a few individuals is the actual textbook definition of prejudice. And implementing policies which profile human beings based on political affiliation, their religious background, and even their skin color (all because those individuals are marketed as having been "radicalized" and are, therefore, a "dangerous demographic") is the definition of institutional prejudice and even, yes, racism. It's the same as it was when our government, media, and ordinary citizens were painting all Muslims with the same broad "terrorist" paintbrush.

The predominant majority of media, newspapers, magazines, and social media "influencers" are repeating these falsehoods, fallacies, associations, lies, and even accusations against entire groups of people, seemingly with impunity and without having to correct or retract a single word. Meanwhile, people who say anything contrary to those establishment narratives run the risk of being considered "in league with potential domestic terrorists"... hence, the current restrictions on speech on social media or otherwise, not to mention the Posse Comitatus-ignoring measures that have been implemented over the course of not only the past week, but over the past year.

This isn't a new phenomenon. These kinds of attempts by the establishment to paint certain people as something which the overwhelming majority are not, is something that's been implemented during the pre-covid era, as well.

If you recall a few years ago, there was a group of students from Covington High School who were in Washington, D.C. for a March for Life rally. They were accused by establishment media and politicians of inciting a racially motivated and aggressive standoff between themselves and Native Americans and African American "Hebrew Israelites." This was done by presenting skewed and out-of-context photos and video clips, making it appear as though the children were aggressors in the situation.

Because of these perceptual/media/political manipulations, there were calls to doxx the students and their families. Pundits and celebrities wanted these students to get punched out, stating that they had very "punchable" faces. The high school even had to be shut down due to death threats against the students, their families, and the school. This was an example of an attempt to ruin the lives, livelihoods, and reputations of individuals for completely fabricated reasons and purely opportunistic political motives.

Thankfully, in the instance of the example I just mentioned, that particular establishment narrative wasn't successful, to the chagrin of those believed and went along with the story; as the families sued for "defamation of character" against the various news outlets, who promoted the deceitful untruths in attempt to ruin the lives of certain individuals… simply because they didn't like their political or religious beliefs. CNN and the Washington Post both paid out hundreds of millions in settlements as a result of the lawsuits.

Keeping this in mind, this might be a good approach to the societal situations regarding the various groups which are being portrayed as, or unfoundedly associated with, "potential violent extremists." The best course of action probably isn't to even attempt any type of protest, because any aspect of it can and will be spun in order to further paint anyone (who can be lumped into the same category) with that same broad brush; and therefore, it will be used as an excuse to smear anyone they want to defame. It might all even be used as an excuse to justify full-on nationwide martial law.

Instead, it might be a better idea for that 1/3 to 1/2 of the population to band together, get some lawyers, and sue the pants off these institutions, media outlets, and celebrities who are trying to ruin the lives, livelihoods, and reputations of anyone who doesn't share the "correct" political or religious beliefs. Using their own legal system against these folks in a peaceful manner might be the way to go. Otherwise, the slander and defamation will continue far into the future… and people who've had nothing to do with (and who will continue to have nothing to do with) any destructive disruptions, will end up paying the price for the few individuals who are unsavory.

Do no harm, but take no crap.

XXI

JOURNAL ENTRY:
JANUARY 20, 2021

In many countries around the world,
the people (or more aptly, "subjects")
of those countries don't understand
the concept of anything other than
absolute power, as that is all they've

ever known. In our own country, people are very quickly forgetting that there is any other way of looking at things as well. Governmental power, corporate power, and pharmaceutical power are not meant to be absolute. They are meant to derive whatever "authority" they pretend to have by means of our consent. In other words, with our "permission." Anything beyond that is coercion. Anything beyond that is harassment. They believe they are allowed to do these things because they are convinced that they possess omnipotent authority. While those who notice, point out, or expose the inconsistencies, the corruption, and the malice; they are only pursuing truth.

XXII

JOURNAL ENTRY:
JANUARY 22, 2021

Former CIA director John Brennan declares that libertarians are the equivalent of a radical insurgency group and therefore, a "threat to our democracy."

He says, "... looks very similar to insurgency movements that we've seen overseas, where they germinate in different parts of the country, and they gain strength. And it brings together an unholy alliance, frequently, of religious extremists, authoritarians, fascists, bigots, racists, nativists, and even libertarians."

These top level officials, who are using the same type rhetoric they used to justify war crimes overseas, are psychotic and delusional.

Where to begin? First of all, "libertarian" is the complete opposite of "authoritarian." Libertarians don't wanna control your lives, that's what people like Brennan want to do. Brennan and his agency toppled foreign governments just for the fun of it, killing millions in the process, and created future generations of pissed off Middle Easterners who vowed revenge; all while funding, arming, and training actual radical extremists to destabilize certain regions… giving our Government an excuse to keep intervening.

Secondly, libertarians are anti-war peace activists who oppose violence on principle; as the keystone of the entire philosophy is called the NAP, or nonaggression principle. So, unless it's a matter of self-defense, we're practically anti-violence to the point of putting Buddhist Monks to shame.

Thirdly, we're a "live and let live" kind of people. In other words, we don't give two shits about skin color, gender, religious affiliation, ethnic background, social status, or anything of the sort. In the words of Dr. MLK, Jr., "...but by the content of their character." Any petty human differences are meaningless.

But, apparently, the truth doesn't matter when it comes to the manufactured narratives which the criminal and genocidal elements of our government wish to propagate. I hate

to break it to you, Brennan, but
libertarians are not America's
equivalent of I S I S, and neither are
the millions of other Americans you
guys are trying to lump together as
one giant "extremist" group.

Don't believe their lies, people.
Think for yourself, for a change. This
sort of thing is how they duped
you into supporting the bombing of
a bunch of impoverished third world
nations, into oblivion.

XXIII

JOURNAL ENTRY:
FEBRUARY 16, 2021

The Sunday Times and other media publications have now falsely claimed that Dr. Jordan Peterson was diagnosed with schizophrenia. This is the kind of example that I'm referring to when I state that mainstream news can get away with making any false claim they want, and never experience any reputational repercussions from it, unlike the people whom they make false claims about: who experience, basically, lifelong ostracism from public credibility, as a result of the headhunting and slanderous nature of "reputable and respectable" news sources.

You can, like Peterson, "listen to the experts" (medical or otherwise), follow their instructions, develope a detrimental autoimmune disorder as a result of their recommendations, have your life nearly ruined; all while you're dealing with your spouse trying her best to survive a rare and deadly form of cancer. Despite this, the mainstream media sources will still have a chip on their shoulder because you won't conform to the societally-pressured, hive-minded groupthink which permeates practically every major institution in daily life anymore. They will (as you have spent nearly two years recovering from said hell) label you as having a severe mental disorder such as schizophrenia in an attempt to further discredit everything you've worked so hard to establish in your life: be it your profession, your publishings, your commentary, your online content, etc… and despite the same media's alleged campaigns to destigmatize mental health issues.

It doesn't matter if you're a clinical psychologist with years of research, study, and access to unlimited credible sources and references which can back up the valid points expressed. They will paint you as just a "crazy drug addict." That is, for some reason, what sticks in the public consciousness, despite the fact that it's a demonstrably manipulative lie; and those slanderous twistings of the truth won't get "fact checked" by "authoritative" sources, nor will there be any retractions in the false narrative they painted. Even if the target of the slander pursues lawsuits against the organizations for their misleading, out of context, tabloid-esque "reporting," it won't even matter… because at that point they've already ruined that person's reputation and their perceived credibility in the public square.

If you happen to express concepts or opinions which aren't considered standard canonical thought among the gatekeepers of acceptable ideas, then you will be painted as a "conspiracy nut." If you happen to have doubts or questions about the legitimacy and validity of American political elections, then you're considered an extremist. If you're among the 74 million people who happened to vote for or support a certain political puppet (which I don't support any, btw), then you are labeled a white nationalist who supports violent insurrections, and are "personally responsible" for an "attempted coup d'etat." If you have valid concerns over governmental policies concerning pandemic protocols and the implications and ramifications for the future of society, then you may be a "threat to the public health" or even a "potential domestic terrorist"... who probably should be on a no-fly-list, put through some sort of "re-education protocol," or even placed via the cdc's shielding approach (i.e. involuntary medical house arrest or other forms of involuntary and indefinite medical detention). If you're a famous individual and discuss historical facts and how they may relate to modern day existence, and you don't happen to have the correct political leanings, then you are allegedly a right wing radical who shouldn't be allowed to make a living as an actor or be able to have a social media account. If you're a libertarian or a classical liberal, then you're apparently no different than an "ISIS enemy combatant."

It doesn't matter how valid or factual the information is, that is presented by any individual. It doesn't matter if what you say is backed up by well sourced documents, articles, or studies. It doesn't matter if you use the mainstream sources, links, and quotes verbatim. It doesn't matter how respectful, respectable, and level-headed you are. If the media and social headhunters decide that you need to face the wrath of their smear campaigns, then you will become a washed up and "discredited" representation of everything wrong, dysfunctional, and evil with humanity.

If all of that is taken as the general rule, then there's really no point in going out of one's way to justify, apologize for, or attempt to convince those who aren't interested in learning, or even actually listening, to the concepts you are trying to address. The purpose of their attempts to purge opposing views doesn't come from a place of understanding an ever-increasing pursuit of truth; due to the dogmatic nature of their own faith, trust, and unquestionable certainty in regards to officials, "experts," and "authority." It comes from a place of closing off critical thinking. It comes from a place of arrogant and almost religious devotion to the status quo of top down authoritarian rationalization. Therefore it is crucial for one to not only be open and strong-minded in the face of such calculated efforts to eliminate points of view… but also to be completely unapologetic in your own personal convictions and your pursuits of unbiased knowledge.

XXIV

JOURNAL ENTRY:
MARCH 1, 2021

People get way too hung up on the "isms" to notice that authoritarianism in all its "variations," whether it's seemingly coming from the far right or the far left, leads to the same consequences for humanity. The ruling classes of civilization have convinced the majority of individuals in modern society that there are two differing and diametrically opposed political paths which folks can get behind…to lead to the best results for a "healthy" society and an effective/productive governing body… and therefore, an alleged maximization of the "common good" for greatest number of people. Those "differing" paths are the "left wing" and the "right wing," and the varying degrees to which ordinary people align themselves with.

The alleged right wing of the spectrum claims to appeal to a "country first" mindset where the interests of the nation, itself, is put above other interests. Now, this can be a benign idea where a government invests in its own people, technology, infrastructure, economic stability, self-reliance, energy independence, etc…and doesn't rely on, nor become entangled with, other nations which may spread their own nation's people and resources too thin. Or… it can be a more dangerous mindset where a government can convince its citizens that other countries or groups are an existential threat to the nation and that, therefore, "We must take action!," preemptively, in order to prevent that threat from trying to destroy "our great nation"…whether it was British Imperialism…or whether it was the Neoconservatives in the Bush, Jr. Administration launching the War on Terror…or whether it was Pinochet's Violent Military Dictatorship in Chile…or whether it was Hitler invading Poland and France and putting Jews into concentration camps…all for "the greater good"…leading to the expansion of an empire.

Meanwhile, the alleged "left wing" of the spectrum claims to appeal to a "collective" and "interdependence" by putting the "needs of everyone" above the "needs of the individual." This can also, fundamentally, be a benign idea where a government invests in people, technology, infrastructure, economic stability, mutual reliance, energy interdependence, etc. Or… it can be a more dangerous mindset where a government can convince its citizens that other countries or groups are an existential threat to the collective and that, therefore, "We must take action!," preemptively, in order to prevent that threat from trying to destroy "our great nation"…whether it was current Democrats fixation on "Russian hackers" or implying that 1/3 of the country is a radical, racist, insurrectionist, terrorist group which needs to be dealt with in the manner of how our government dealt with Al Qaeda and ISIS…or whether it was FDR putting law abiding Japanese Americans in internment camps simply because of their ethnic background.. or whether it's the Soviet Union's GULAG…or whether it's China's violent "cultural revolution," or their social crediting system, or their internment of ethnic/religious minorities, or their violent takeover of peaceful regions like Tibet…all for "the greater good" and leading to the expansion of empire.

Both of the alleged "wings" of political loyalties base themselves on the premise of the State solving the problems facing humanity. The problem is that, more often than not, it is the State itself which is causing the problems facing humanity… and both of these "wings" taken to their logical extremes.. results in humanity ending up in the same pickle: consolidation for a very few powerful, overarching, and overreaching oligarchs… and the repression, subjugation, imprisonment, and often the extermination of vast numbers of ordinary people.

So, when it comes down to it… the different "ism" labels we place on these various concepts don't really matter. The word "Nazi" itself literally means "National Socialism"… or when expanded, "National Socialist German Workers' Party." I don't think that history books labeling Hitler either a "right wing" extremist or a "left wing" extremist is really much consolation to the millions who were placed in concentration camps and exterminated by those genocidal lunatics.

Similarly, the Chinese government calls its nation the "People's Republic of China." It's obviously not a republic, nor do "the people" have any say over how the government operates. It's not like they get to vote, or express their concerns, or criticize policies, or petition for a redress of grievances. If someone does any of that... they're imprisoned, reeducated, or executed. I don't think it's of any consequence to those who've been oppressed by the CCP as to which wing of the governmental bird is holding them in bondage, let alone what "ism" people have ascribed to it.

As far as the individual cult-of-personality figures, which people tend to rally behind in support or opposition of, they generally serve to keep those people (who've bought into the division of the left/right political paradigm) focused on each other and the "evils" of each other's "wing"... so they don't notice that both wings are trapping everyone under the same bird of prey.

In the case of Trump, think of him like a governmental version of Alex Jones in regard to what societal purpose and function was served by him being in office for four years. Whereas the idea of an "Alex Jones" made it possible for those in positions of power and their social media arm of Silicon Valley to (at least at first) paint anyone who questioned the narratives and motives of governmental policies and media as "tinfoil hat wearing conspiracy nuts."

Well, the idea of Trump has allowed those in power and the media paint anyone who supported Trump as a "white nationalist insurrectionist." It doesn't even have to be Trump supporters anymore, as it can be anyone who questions the government's motives behind Covid policies, or people who are critical of U.S. government's foreign policy, or people who don't believe in the fiction that elections in this country are "fair" and "immune from large scale tampering"… unless, of course, those dang ol' Russian hackers are "meddling in our elections" again. It is simply a historical "fact" in that case. *sarcasm*

One has to keep in mind that the fundamental changes that have taken place in this country over the past year were allowed to transpire by Trump's administration. His agencies, his advisors, his appointed experts, and the media kept everyone focused on "Trump's responsibility" for the devastation, deaths, and carnage that transpired in 2020. Meanwhile people from all walks of life were at each other's throats and pointing blame at one another as the largest consolidation of global power (and the largest wealth transfer in human history) was seized upon and exploited by world organizations which have no loyalty to any nation, constitution, or people.

They were able to socially engineer the behaviors, policies, concerns, and interpersonal relationships of practically any person and nation around the world overnight… literally just by speaking it into existence. "No time for questions. No time for debate. Do what you're told now or pay the consequences." That is the motto for modern civilization.

Unfortunately, seemingly smaller and even inconsequential elements of this logic and social conditioning was done by Trump, himself, even though it's not brought up very often. It's merely been a continuation of incrementally stripping individuals of fundamental and constitutionally protected rights which began long before Trump ever took office… and will continue under Biden's administration, and even further into the future.

As far as the free speech issue… in December of 2019, Trump signed an executive order in effect banning criticism of the Israeli Government on college campuses by labeling it an effort to "combat antisemitism." However, using one's speech to criticize or boycott a government is not akin to hating individuals based on ethnicity or religion. So, in effect, he did censor free speech. It just wasn't focused on by the media because Trump is supposed to be a "Nazi," right? Well, real Nazis hate Jews, or others, because of their ethnicity and religion. Nazis don't combat antisemitism. Therefore, that doesn't fit the narrative… so, why would the media focus on that?

As far as gun control…Trump banned bump stocks, supported Red Flag laws, and even stated, "Take the guns first, go through due process second." However, no one really wants to talk about that either.

And as I stressed earlier, the implementation of restrictions in practically every aspect of human life (in this country) was allowed during Trump's presidency. As a result, now people have been conditioned to believe that governments taking over every aspect of life under certain pretenses are necessary and crucial for the fabric of society. Apparently, unless we grant them authority over every action engaged by ordinary people, we will be on the precipice of extinction… because I guess people are just too simple minded to make their own decisions and, therefore, can't be left to their own devices. *sarcasm*

Government has even subtly convinced people in this country, yet again, that it may be necessary to put those "suspected" of being a "public health risk" into special medical detention centers for the sake of "preventing the spread of illness."

It's convinced people that certain differing views, opinions, thoughts, and expressions are tantamount to "violent extremism." They do this to justify their censorship, suppression, and banning… due to the tireless efforts of Big Tech corporations. It's to the point where having the "wrong" opinion on something can result in a person being ostracized by friends, family, or community. It could even get you on a no-fly list, or worse, simply because of subjective interpretations, misreadings, or deliberately misleading and out-of-context analyses of whatever the subject matter may be.

I, for one, don't really care which "ism" it is that governments happen to be using at any given time for their divide-and-conquer extracurricular activities. It's not a liberalism versus conservatism thing. It's not a socialism versus capitalism thing. It's not a communism versus fascism thing. It's not a black versus white thing. When it comes down to it… it's only an authoritarian versus humanity thing. To hell with the two wings on the Big Government Bird of Prey.

XXV

CONCLUSION

In my opinion, the world is turning into a global dystopian hellscape before our very eyes. Many folks have been warning others of these types of scenarios for years and years. Yet, people keep rolling along with it. They will roll up their sleeves, offer up their nostrils, and relinquish every one of their innate freedoms. I'd guess probably half the population have been brainwashed into thinking that these are all good things "to combat illness and death." Their lives, their humanity, their freedom, and their children's future are on the line at this point.

People have been lulled into subservience. I really don't think it's possible to wake the majority of people up anymore. I think anything said by us truth-seekers is merely preaching to the choir. Everyone else probably just rolls their eyes and thinks, "Ugh, there goes them damn conspiracy theorists again." I, and many others, have been figuratively screaming from the rooftops that these things were very likely to happen, even before the first set of lockdowns happened last March. Yet, people just wanted to argue with us, downplay what we were saying, and compare it all to a belief in "flat earth" or "reptilian overlords."

I've said this before, but people will literally be defending governments' actions until the moment folks are shoved into the gas chambers. Hopefully it doesn't come to that before people peaceably take back their own humanity.

AFTERWORD

BY FRANC TURNER

In short, this is all about a 100% takeover of any and all human autonomy, one giant step at a time. It's never been about anyone's health or saving lives. They want to orchestrate more and more crises in order to elicit more and more dependence on the State. Anything doled out by the oligarchs, at this point, will have infinite strings attached, which will strangle every last breath of true liberty... liberty that has been taken for granted for the past several decades. Compliance breeds despotism. Noncompliance breeds independence. As far as all of these current events go...the State, Big Pharma, and Big Business aren't going to stop anytime soon. If anything, they're going to double down. They're gonna make life harder and harder for those of us who have even the most rudimentary understanding of what's really going on. We're going to have to keep peaceably standing our ground while not allowing ourselves to cave in to any aspect of what they throw at us. This nightmare ends because we say it does, not because those at the top give anyone "permission" to live life as an unimpeded human being. Stay strong, stay safe, stay vigilant, and above all else... Live Free!

ACKNOWLEDGEMENTS

The content within is observations, rants, and satirical musings written by myself between 2020 and 2021 for entertainment purposes. First and foremost, I'd like to thank my late parents. They were always extremely loving, encouraging, and supportive of everything I'd ever done, whether it was music, writing, or whatever else I'd put my mind to. More importantly, they always inspired me to stand up for what I believe in, and to speak out against injustices. I'd like to thank my friend and fellow writer, researcher, and truth seeker, Steve Cameron. You're an inspiration, and your resilience and tenacity are something that other people should strive for. I'd like to give special thanks to Donald Jeffries for his outspokenness and bravery in the fields of truth and research. I'd like to thank Steve Ary and his newspaper, The Vanderburgh Independent Press; or The VIP News. Several of my writings presented in this book were first published in The VIP News under my column titled, "The Rant." I'm also very thankful for your encouragement and for your appreciation of my writings. The sections which first appeared in The VIP News are as follows: March 15, 2020; April 12, 2020; April 21, 2020; August 15, 2020; October 15, 2020; January 19, 2021; March 1, 2021. I'd also like to thank my friends at Ask A Libertarian for giving me my first article publications in years past: Jared, Kris M., Travis, Lyssa. You guys are great! I'd like to thank my friends and close acquaintances who've enjoyed my rants, commentary, and articles.. and who've encouraged me to stick with it and to go even further. You all know who you are, but namely: Steve T.,

Steve E., Mr. Bill, Matt M., Roni, Cory, Jess, Christy B., Liz M., Mikey, Nick, Peter, Vicki, Judi W., John L., Kris I., Terry, Josh, Kyle, Linda T., etc. I love you all, and thank you so very much!

-Franc Turner

PHOTO CREDITS

Page 9: Steve Cameron: "Headlines" (August 2021); p. 11: Program for the silent movie: "Danserindens Kærlighedsdrøm" (DK/US: 1916); p. 15: "The orchestra and its instruments" (Richard Strauss conducting: 1917); p. 19: Unknown; p. 23: Steve Cameron: "Epstein Didn't Kill Himself" (August 2021); p. 29: Unknown; p. 31: Steve Cameron: "Line In The Sand" (August 2021); p. 37: Carlos Pacheco: "Stanley Kubrick Exhibition" (2015, creativecommons.org/licenses/by/4.0); p. 41: Unknown; p. 49: Carlos Ruiz (creativecommons.org/licenses/by/4.0); p. 53: Beverly Hills Police Department: "BHPD riot cops"; p. 57: Hawken King: "V for Vendetta" (creativecommons.org/licenses/by/4.0); p. 63: The White House: "President Trump at Davos" (January 21, 2020); p. 67: Frank Gualtieri: "The Three Wise Monkeys, carving on the stable of Tosho-gu Shrine, Nikko, Japan" (2005); p. 73: National Park Service: "September 11th Attacks" (September 11, 2001); p. 75: Steve Cameron: "Money" (August 2021); p. 81: Franc Turner: "Cancelled Christmas" (August 2021); p. 85: Tyler Merbler: "Storming of the United States Capitol" (January 6, 2021, creativecommons.org/licenses/by/4.0); p. 89: Department of State of the United States of America: "Colin Powell official Secretary of State" (January 1, 2001); p. 95: Sgt. Brian R. Calhoun: "South Carolina National Guard supports 59th Presidential Inauguration" (January 20, 2021); p. 101: Allen & Co: "Picture of John Dalberg-Acton, 1st Baron Acton" (1902); p. 103: Franc Turner: "Libertarian Definition" (August 2021); p. 107: Gage Skidmore: "Jordan Peterson speaking with attendees at the 2018

Student Action Summit" (December 20, 2018, creativecommons.org/licenses/by/4.0); p. 113: Steve Cameron: "Keep Left/Right" (August 2021); p. 123: Franc Turner: "1984" (August 2021); Front Cover Image: Navyatha123: "Photo of the Constitution of the United States of America" (October 2006, creativecommons.org/licenses/by/4.0)

More titles from Steve Cameron Productions:

THE DEPUTY INTERVIEWS:
THE TRUE STORY OF J.F.K. ASSASSINATION
WITNESS, AND FORMER DALLAS DEPUTY SHERIFF,
ROGER DEAN CRAIG

**by Steve Cameron (Author), David Ratcliffe
(Foreword), Phil Singer (Preface)**

The Deputy Interviews: The True Story of J.F.K. Assassination Witness, and Former Dallas Deputy Sheriff, Roger Dean Craig by Steve Cameron, is a book of interviews conducted with JFK assassination experts, insiders, & family members who knew former Dallas Deputy Sheriff Roger Dean Craig, who witnessed numerous events that occurred in Dealey Plaza on November 22, 1963, that dramatically contradict the Warren Commission's final conclusions about the J.F.K. assassination.

Publisher: Steve Cameron Productions
Language: English
Paperback: 316 pages
Available in paperback & eBook at Amazon & other online retailers
Signed author copies available at:
stevecameronproductions.com

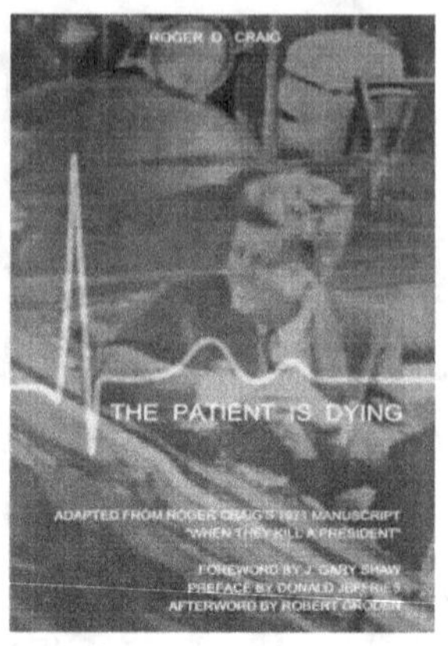

THE PATIENT IS DYING: ADAPTED FROM ROGER CRAIG'S 1971 MANUSCRIPT "WHEN THEY KILL A PRESIDENT"
by Roger D. Craig (Author), J. Gary Shaw (Foreword), Donald Jeffries (Preface), Rita Musgrove (Introduction), Robert J. Groden (Afterword)

Steve Cameron's new companion piece to his groundbreaking book *The Deputy Interviews*. *The Patient Is Dying* includes new material, including a foreword written by first generation JFK assassination researcher and author, J. Gary Shaw (*Cover-up, JFK: Conspiracy of Silence, Trauma Room One*), a preface written by best- selling author Donald Jeffries (*Survival of the Richest, Hidden History, Bullyocracy*), and an afterword written by world-renowned JFK assassination researcher and author, Robert J. Groden (*JFK: The Case For Conspiracy, The Killing of a President, JFK: Absolute proof*).

Publisher: Steve Cameron Productions
Language: English
Paperback: 122 pages
Available in paperback & eBook at Amazon & other online retailers
Signed author copies available at:
stevecameronproductions.com

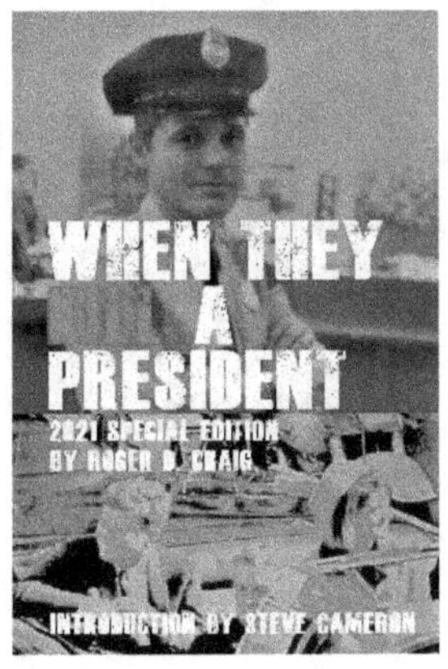

"WHEN THEY KILL A PRESIDENT"
by Roger D. Craig (Author), Steve Cameron (Introduction)
A companion piece to Steve Cameron's groundbreaking book *The Deputy Interviews*, *When They Kill A President* was originally a an unpublished manuscript written in 1971 by Roger Dean Craig, a decorated Dallas Deputy Sheriff who won 'Officer of the Year' for Dallas County in 1960 for outstanding performance in the line of duty. This new 2021 Special Edition of Craig's manuscript documents his eyewitness account of the assassination of President John F. Kennedy, his investigation in Dealey Plaza after it occurred, and the massive cover up that followed. This first-hand account of what took place in Dallas on November 22, 1963, proves not only that there was a vast conspiracy to kill John F. Kennedy, but it also examines how costly telling the truth could be for an eyewitness like Roger Craig, who threatened to expose the lies of the official narrative surrounding the assassination of the 35th President of the United States.

Publisher: Steve Cameron Productions
Language: English
Paperback: 100 pages
Available in paperback & eBook at Amazon & other online retailers
Signed author copies available at:
stevecameronproductions.com

www.ingramcontent.com/pod-product-compliance
Lightning Source LLC
Chambersburg PA
CBHW061641250726
48659CB00004B/1332